THE WORLD OF OCEAN ANIMALS
NARWHALS

by Mari Schuh

POGO

Ideas for Parents and Teachers

Pogo Books let children practice reading informational text while introducing them to nonfiction features such as headings, labels, sidebars, maps, and diagrams, as well as a table of contents, glossary, and index.

Carefully leveled text with a strong photo match offers early fluent readers the support they need to succeed.

Before Reading

• "Walk" through the book and point out the various nonfiction features. Ask the student what purpose each feature serves.

• Look at the glossary together. Read and discuss the words.

Read the Book

• Have the child read the book independently.

• Invite him or her to list questions that arise from reading.

After Reading

• Discuss the child's questions. Talk about how he or she might find answers to those questions.

• Prompt the child to think more. Ask: Narwhals live in Arctic waters. What other animals live in the Arctic?

Pogo Books are published by Jump!
5357 Penn Avenue South
Minneapolis, MN 55419
www.jumplibrary.com

Library of Congress Cataloging-in-Publication Data

Names: Schuh, Mari C., 1975- author.
Title: Narwhals / by Mari Schuh.
Description: Minneapolis, MN: Jump!, Inc., [2022]
Series: The world of ocean animals
Includes index. | Audience: Ages 7-10
Identifiers: LCCN 2020055080 (print)
LCCN 2020055081 (ebook)
ISBN 9781636900605 (hardcover)
ISBN 9781636900612 (paperback)
ISBN 9781636900629 (ebook)
Subjects: LCSH: Narwhal—Juvenile literature.
Classification: LCC QL737.C433 .S384 2022 (print)
LCC QL737.C433 (ebook) | DDC 599.5/43—dc23
LC record available at https://lccn.loc.gov/2020055080
LC ebook record available at https://lccn.loc.gov/2020055081

Editor: Jenna Gleisner
Designer: Michelle Sonnek

Photo Credits: dottedhippo/iStock, cover; by wildestanimal/Getty, 1; Flip Nicklin/Minden Pictures/SuperStock, 3, 5, 16-17, 19; Todd Mintz/Alamy, 4, 14-15; Bryan and Cherry Alexander/Nature Picture Library, 6-7; Eric Baccega/Nature Picture Library, 8-9; Doug Allan/Nature Picture Library, 10-11; Franco Banfi/WaterF/Age Fotostock, 12; Bluegreen Pictures/SuperStock, 13; All Canada Photos/Alamy, 18, 23; Animals Animals/SuperStock, 20-21.

Printed in the United States of America at Corporate Graphics in North Mankato, Minnesota.

TABLE OF CONTENTS

CHAPTER 1

TUSKS AND BLUBBER

A spotted whale swims in the icy ocean. Its long tusk sticks out of the water. What is this whale? It's a narwhal!

tusk

Narwhals have black and white patches on their skin. The skin on their bellies is lighter. Their color can change over time. Older narwhals might be all white.

Narwhals are born with two teeth. In males and some females, one tooth grows into a **hollow** tusk.

Tusks have **spiral** grooves and are covered in tiny holes. The holes let in water. Scientists think this might help narwhals feel changes in water temperature. This could help them find **prey**. They may also use their tusks to hunt.

DID YOU KNOW?

Because of their tusks, narwhals are sometimes called unicorns of the sea. Tusks can grow to about 9 feet (2.7 meters) long. They can weigh more than 20 pounds (9.1 kilograms).

Narwhals live in the Arctic. They swim in rivers and water near the **coast**. The water is icy and cold. It is also very dark. This makes it hard for scientists to study them.

TAKE A LOOK!

Take a look at where narwhals live. Why do you think the water is cold and icy?

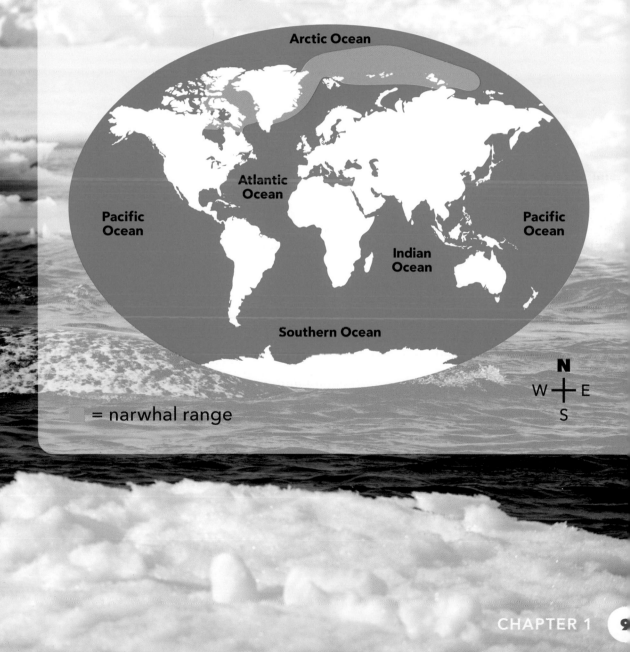

Arctic Ocean

Atlantic Ocean

Pacific Ocean

Pacific Ocean

Indian Ocean

Southern Ocean

N
W — E
S

= narwhal range

Like most marine **mammals**, narwhals have a layer of **blubber**. It keeps them warm. They use their flippers and **flukes** to move in the water. They swim slowly.

TAKE A LOOK!

What are a narwhal's body parts called? Take a look!

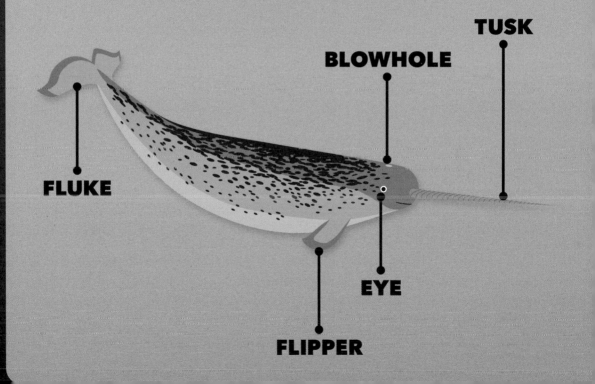

TUSK

BLOWHOLE

FLUKE

EYE

FLIPPER

CHAPTER 2

SURVIVING IN THE ARCTIC

Narwhals eat a lot during the winter. They dive deep to find food. It is dark!

They eat fish, squid, and shrimp.
They suck the prey into their mouths.
Then they swallow it whole. Gulp!

squid

blowhole

A narwhal can stay underwater for about 25 minutes. Then it comes up for air. It breathes through a **blowhole**.

Sheets of ice shift and move. Narwhals are slow swimmers. They can get stuck under big, moving ice sheets. This makes them easy targets for **predators**. Sharks and orcas eat narwhals. Polar bears and walruses do, too.

DID YOU KNOW?

A narwhal's biggest threat is people. **Pollution** and hunting harm narwhals. **Climate change** does, too. It causes temperatures to rise. This creates more moving ice.

ice sheet

CHAPTER 3

MIGRATING MAMMALS

Narwhals travel in groups called **pods**. Pods often have 15 to 20 narwhals. Some pods have hundreds or thousands!

In the spring, they **migrate** north. They swim to shallow waters without ice. They live there during the summer.

calf

Females give birth in the spring as they migrate. A female usually has one **calf** at a time. Calves are born gray. A calf drinks its mother's milk for at least one year. It will spend its life in the cold, icy water of the Arctic.

ACTIVITIES & TOOLS

MEASURE A NARWHAL

See how you compare to the lengths of narwhal adults and calves with this fun activity!

What You Need:
- driveway or sidewalk
- chalk
- tape measure, yardstick, or meterstick
- adult or friend

❶ Find a driveway or sidewalk that is flat, clean, and safe.

❷ Use chalk and a tape measure to draw a line that is 20 feet (6.1 meters) long. This is about the length of an adult narwhal.

❸ Now draw a line that is 5 feet (1.5 meters) long. This is about the length of a narwhal calf.

❹ Lie down near the line for the adult narwhal. Have an adult or friend measure you and make a mark to show your length. How does your length compare? See how many of your body lengths equal the length of an adult narwhal.

❺ Do the same next to the line for the calf. How does your length compare?

GLOSSARY

blowhole: The nostril on the top of a whale or dolphin head that is used for breathing air.

blubber: A thick layer of fat under the skin of some ocean animals.

calf: A young narwhal.

climate change: Changes in Earth's weather and climate over time.

coast: The land next to an ocean or sea.

flukes: The wide, flat parts of a narwhal's tail.

hollow: Empty inside.

mammals: Warm-blooded animals that give birth to live young, which drink milk from their mothers.

migrate: To travel from one place to another place during different times of the year.

pods: Groups of narwhals.

pollution: Harmful materials that damage or contaminate the air, water, or soil.

predators: Animals that hunt other animals for food.

prey: Animals that are hunted by other animals for food.

spiral: Winding in a continuous curve around a fixed point.

INDEX

TO LEARN MORE

Finding more information is as easy as 1, 2, 3.

❶ Go to www.factsurfer.com

❷ Enter "narwhals" into the search box.

❸ Choose your book to see a list of websites.

FACT SURFER